Thank you to the children who suggested their favourite
amazing facts: Tom Bourne-Cox, Lyra Chilton, Rudy
Chilton, Calla Mackenzie, Evan Mackenzie — C.B.

For George and Lily – S.J.

Written by Catherine Brereton.
Illustrations by Steve James.
Front cover design by Thy Bui.
Red Shed would also like to thank author Clive Gifford and
illustrator Chris Dickason for use of some content from *Fake News.*

First published in Great Britain in 2021 by Red Shed, part of Farshore

An imprint of HarperCollins*Publishers*
1 London Bridge Street, London SE1 9GF
www.farshore.co.uk

HarperCollins*Publishers*
1st Floor, Watermarque Building, Ringsend Road, Dublin 4, Ireland

Copyright © HarperCollins*Publishers* Limited 2021

ISBN 978 0 0084 9219 9
001
Printed and Bound in the UK using 100% Renewable Electricity
at CPI Group (UK) Ltd.

A CIP catalogue is available from the British Library.

Stay safe online. Any website addresses listed in this book are correct at the time of going
to print. However, Farshore is not responsible for content hosted by third parties. Please be
aware that online content can be subject to change and websites can contain content that is
unsuitable for children. We advise that all children are supervised when using the internet.

MIX
Paper from
responsible sources
FSC™ C007454

AMAZING FACTS
EVERY 8 YEAR OLD
NEEDS TO KNOW

RED SHED

Whether you love animals or adventure, science or sport, you'll find LOADS of weird and wonderful facts ...

How many different bacteria are there in your gut?

What bird uses sick as a weapon?

Where would you find a real-life unicorn?

Where did football fans cause an earthquake?

Read on to find out the answers and lots more awesome information ...

Snakes sometimes have two heads.

It was double trouble for a pet cat that found a two-headed racer snake in Florida, United States, in 2020.

If a starfish loses an arm it can regrow it.

It might lose the arm to escape a predator or just to keep cool. The lost arm can sometimes even grow into a whole new body!

Bullfrogs can sick up their whole stomach.

Many animals vomit the contents of their
stomach if they eat something poisonous, but
the bullfrog can bring up its whole stomach.
This also scares off predators.

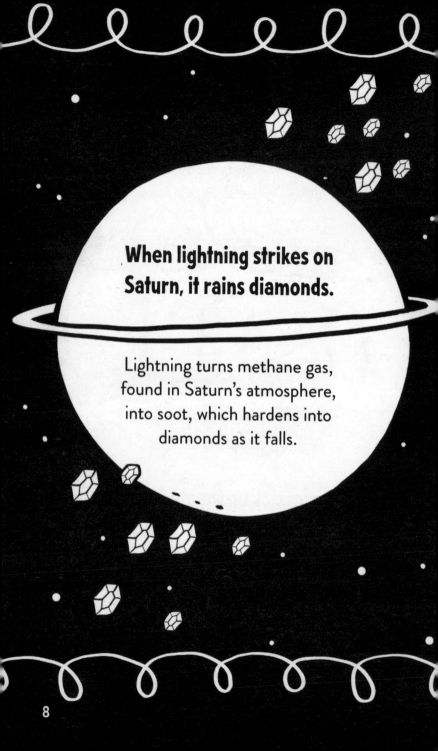

When lightning strikes on Saturn, it rains diamonds.

Lightning turns methane gas, found in Saturn's atmosphere, into soot, which hardens into diamonds as it falls.

If you could make a bath big enough, Saturn would float in it!

The giant planet is made of gas and is lighter than water.

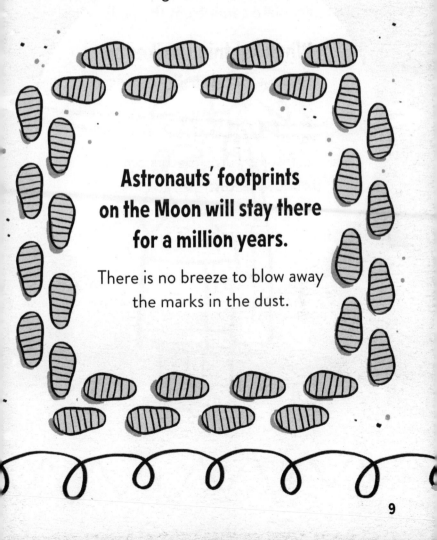

Astronauts' footprints on the Moon will stay there for a million years.

There is no breeze to blow away the marks in the dust.

The Aztec emperor Montezuma drank 50 cups of chocolate every day!

The Aztecs (who lived in Central America in the 14th to 16th centuries) thought chocolate came from the gods.

The Aztecs played a game similar to basketball.

The game was played on a stone court and players had to get a solid rubber ball through a stone ring.

Some male penguins give females rocks as presents.

The rock gifts are meant to impress the female,
and she'll use them to build her nest.

A group of penguins is called a waddle.

They can walk – or waddle –
over very long distances.

Penguins cannot fly,
but they can jump!

Penguins use their wings to swim fast
underwater. If they want to get up in the air,
though, Adélie penguins can leap up to 2m high
out of the water and on to ice or land.

Queen Victoria was the first monarch ever to ride on a train.

She made the 32-km journey in 1842 in her own royal carriage. A few years later, her carriage was the first in the world to have its own toilet.

Queen Elizabeth II is a trained truck mechanic.

When she was young, the then Princess Elizabeth joined the military and learned to change tyres, fix trucks and drive them.

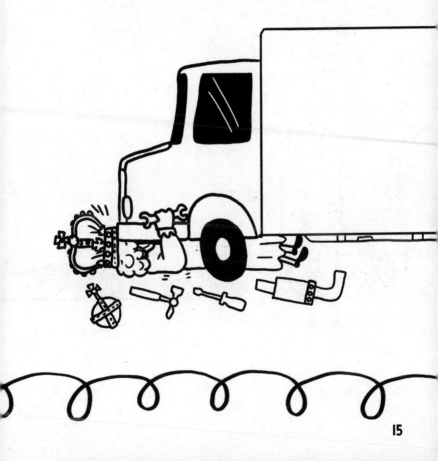

Honey can last more than 3,000 years without going bad.

The ancient Egyptian tomb of Tutankhamun contains pots of honey that are still good enough to eat.

Archaeologists also discovered mummified boxes of meat in Tutankhamun's tomb – but you wouldn't want to eat those!

Other well-past-it ancient food discoveries include 3,000-year-old butter in Ireland, 4,000-year-old noodles in China and 14,400-year old pitta bread in Jordan!

Honey is easy to digest because bees have already partly digested it for you.

A honeybee eats nectar, then starts to break down the nectar's sugars in its honey stomach before it stores and dries the nectar in the hive to make honey.

**Sir David Attenborough has
several different animals
and plants named after him.**

There's a miniature spider,
a carnivorous plant, a rainforest
flower, a butterfly, a little yellow
wildflower and a blue Australian
lizard. Then there's a prehistoric
grasshopper, a prehistoric fish and
a prehistoric sea reptile . . . called
Attenborosaurus, of course!

All the cows in the world produce enough gas to inflate 150,000 airships every day.

There are around a billion cows on the planet and each can produce 500l of methane gas every day from burping, farting and pooing.

Bulls are NOT enraged by the colour red.

Bulls are actually colour-blind. When a bullfighter waves a red cape in front of a bull, the animal is irritated or angered only by the movement, not the colour.

Mother llamas hum to their babies (which are called crias).

And male llamas make a gurgling noise or scream at each other if they're fighting, or make loud shrieks of alarm if they see danger coming.

Llamas spit to settle an argument!

They're normally very calm, gentle animals, but if they're arguing over food or want to tell another llama to go away, they fire off a shot of spit.

Llamas are well adapted to living high up in the mountains.

They have thick, warm fur and their blood is suited to letting them breathe in the thin mountain air. Like their cousins, camels, they don't need to drink much water either.

At the Lehe Ledu Wildlife Zoo in Chongqing, China, visitors pay to be locked in cages.

They watch from inside the cages as lions, tigers and bears roam outside. Chunks of meat tied onto the outside of the cage tempt the animals up close!

Baby Leopard

Baby Lion

A newborn baby leopard has no spots.

At birth the tiny cub is grey and fluffy
with fuzzy markings that develop into spots.
By contrast, baby lions start life with sandy
spots, but soon lose them.

The long jump for horses was once an Olympic sport.

At the 1900 Olympic Games in Paris, France, a horse called Extra Dry won a gold medal by landing a jump of 6.10m.

Other strange events at the same Olympic Games included tug of war and croquet.

Wilt 'The Stilt' Chamberlain once scored 100 points in a single basketball game.

Many basketball games end with scorelines of 90–84 or 88–76 but Chamberlain scored 100 points all by himself, helping his Philadelphia Warriors beat the New York Knicks in 1962.

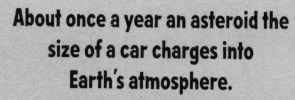

About once a year an asteroid the size of a car charges into Earth's atmosphere.

Asteroids are space rocks that whizz around in space and sometimes crash into planets. Luckily for us on Earth, they usually burn up before they reach the ground.

If you could drive to the Moon in an ordinary car, it would take 168½ days.

That's at a speed of 95km/h, driving non-stop. In 1969 the first men to land on the Moon got there in their spaceship in 76 hours.

Packets of crisps are kept fresh with a puff of the gas nitrogen inside.

The inventor of Pringles is buried in a Pringles tube.

American scientist Fredric Baur invented the method of stacking and packaging the curved crisps in 1966. He was so proud of his invention that he wanted his ashes to be buried in a Pringles can.

Weird crisp flavours around the world include octopus, cappuccino, white chocolate and peppermint, kiwi fruit and cola!

Most British crisps have their best before date on a Saturday.

It's down to how the factory works. At Walkers Crisps factories, everything made in a particular week has the same expiry date. And it happens to be a Saturday – check for yourself!

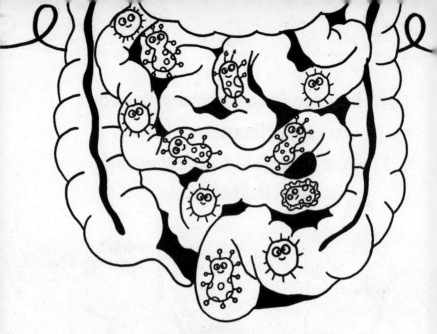

More than half the cells in your body aren't human.

They are outnumbered by the billions and trillions of bacteria, fungi, viruses and microscopic creatures that call YOU their home.

Your gut alone contains 300–500 DIFFERENT kinds of bacteria.

Some are harmful and cause disease, but many help digest your food and even keep you healthy.

Every second, your body makes 25 million new cells.

Most of them are so small that about 10,000 could fit on a pinhead.

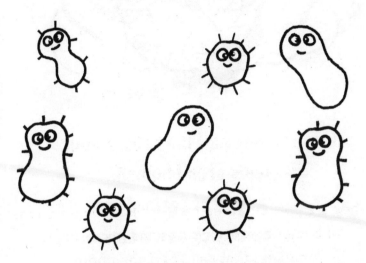

The longest cells in your body are nerve cells.

Nerve cells can be as little as 0.001mm wide but a metre long! Signals zip along them at 420km/h.

A type of seabird uses chick sick as a weapon.

The bird, called a fulmar, has a super-smelly oil in its stomach. When a predator comes near, it spews out a disgusting-smelling stream of sick to send the enemy packing.

The largest flower in the world is also one of the smelliest.

The rafflesia is a giant red rainforest flower that measures around a metre across. It smells like rotting meat!

Shark skin is like a cheese grater.

Sharks have scaly skin and the scales
are hard, rough and triangular – like
little pointy teeth all over their body.

Baby sand tiger sharks eat their brothers and sisters.

What's more, they do it before they're even born! These sharks hatch inside their mother's body, and the biggest one eats all its siblings before it emerges from its mother.

Some sharks can see with their eyes shut.

They do this because of see-through inner eyelids called 'nicitating' eyelids. They shut these to protect their eyes, for example if they are attacking prey.

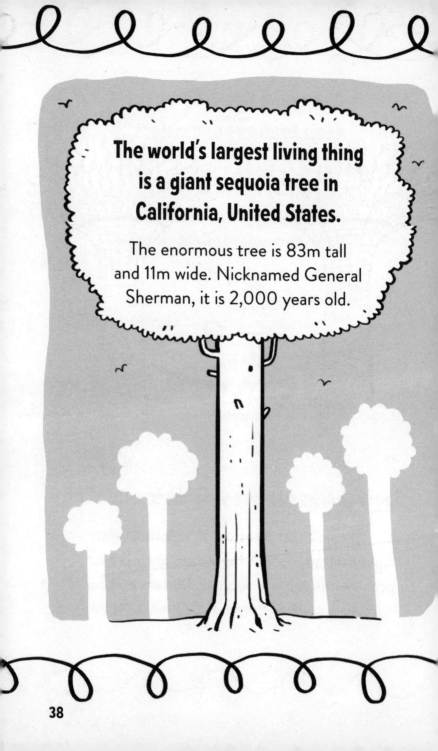

The world's largest living thing is a giant sequoia tree in California, United States.

The enormous tree is 83m tall and 11m wide. Nicknamed General Sherman, it is 2,000 years old.

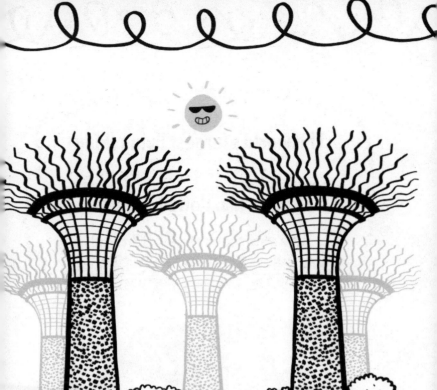

In Singapore there is a beautiful forest of 'supertrees'.

The artificial trees work as solar power generators, collect rainwater, absorb heat, provide shelter and support flowers and ferns growing on them. Rather like real trees do!

Julius Caesar was once captured by pirates.

In 75BCE, some time before he became emperor, Caesar was seized by pirates. The villains got more than they bargained for though, as after he was freed he got together a fleet to capture them, and had them all executed.

Romans wrote bad reviews of places to eat, just like people do today.

"This food is poison" and "you sell us water but keep the good wine for yourself" are just two examples of graffiti found in the ancient Roman city of Pompeii, Italy.

Caesar salad is NOT named after Julius Caesar.

It's not even an ancient dish. It's thought to have been invented in 1924 by an Italian chef, Caesar Cardini, in the town of Tijuana, Mexico.

In a classic April Fool's joke, a BBC TV documentary showed spaghetti growing on trees!

In 1957, viewers in Britain were astonished to watch Swiss farmers gathering in their annual spaghetti harvest – from trees! Back then, people in Britain were not so familiar with pasta, so many of them believed it.

Scientists have taught spinach to send emails.

Spinach roots can detect when there are traces of explosives in underground water, and they give off a signal. Engineers in the United States have invented a way for a camera to read the signal and send an email alert.

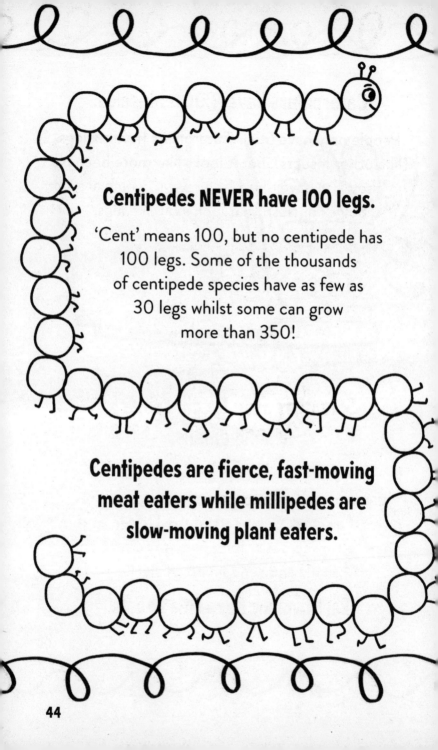

Centipedes **NEVER** have 100 legs.

'Cent' means 100, but no centipede has 100 legs. Some of the thousands of centipede species have as few as 30 legs whilst some can grow more than 350!

Centipedes are fierce, fast-moving meat eaters while millipedes are slow-moving plant eaters.

Caterpillars have 4,000 muscles.

People only have 650. Caterpillars have six legs (like other insects), but it looks like more because they also have up to 10 'prolegs', which are bulges of flesh that look a bit like legs.

Earthworms have five hearts.

In 2021, US President Joe Biden's dogs Major and Champ became the latest pets to move into the White House.

Previous presidential pets include Barack Obama's dogs Sunny and Bo, Bill Clinton's cat Socks and George W. Bush's dog Barney.

And there have been some unusual choices: John Quincy Adams kept an alligator, Abraham Lincoln kept goats, Calvin Coolidge kept a pygmy hippo and Theodore Roosevelt kept two bear cubs.

Elephants can predict the future.

That's what happened on the island of
Sumatra, Indonesia, in 2004. Elephants
near the sea started trumpeting and
heading for the hills. Soon afterwards,
an enormous tsunami hit the coast.

And goats know when something's about to blow . . .

In 2011, scientists noticed that goats living on the slopes of Mount Etna, a volcano in Italy, got nervous and jumpy just before the volcano erupted.

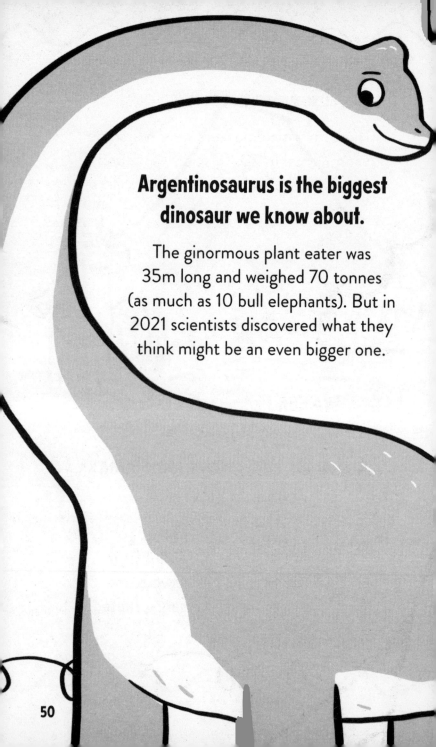

Argentinosaurus is the biggest dinosaur we know about.

The ginormous plant eater was 35m long and weighed 70 tonnes (as much as 10 bull elephants). But in 2021 scientists discovered what they think might be an even bigger one.

Allosauruses may have eaten each other.

These Jurassic dinosaurs were fearsome carnivores. In 2020, scientists found fossil *Allosaurus* bones with bite marks made by . . . other *Allosauruses*!

We don't know what colour dinosaurs were.

Fossils don't preserve colour so we have to guess, based on animals today. Some were probably dull-coloured for camouflage and others bright to attract mates or warn off predators.

A man has been driving his taxi backwards for over 15 years.

Harpreet Devi's taxi got stuck in reverse gear in Bhatinda, India, in 2003 and he didn't have the money to fix it, so he carried on driving in reverse . . . and has done so ever since!

The world's longest car has 26 wheels.

It is a luxury stretch limousine, 30m long with a swimming pool inside and a helicopter landing pad on the back!

Scotland's national animal is the unicorn.

It was chosen by King William I of Scotland in the 12th century, because people believed that unicorns were the strongest animals of all.

The Loch Ness Monster was first spotted nearly 1,500 years ago, by St Columba.

The monster, known as Nessie, is a legendary beast said to roam the deep waters of Scotland's Loch Ness. A famous photo taken in 1933 turned out to be the trunk of an elephant from a nearby circus.

Monsters like the Loch Ness Monster are said to have been seen in Canada's Lake Okanagan and Africa's Congo river.

The Ogopogo in Canada and Mokele-mbembe in the Congo are sometimes thought to be dinosaur-like monsters that have somehow survived. There is probably a much less mysterious explanation, although no one has completely solved the puzzle.

Japanese has a word – tsundoko – for buying books and never getting round to reading them.

A hotel in Nagasaki, Japan, has robot staff members.

The robots recognise guests' faces, carry their bags and clean the rooms. But after a few years the hotel sacked half the robots because guests preferred real people . . . and the robots kept breaking down.

Viking helmets did NOT have horns, and the Vikings weren't all bloodthirsty invaders.

Dozens of Viking helmets have been discovered by archaeologists and none have horns. And while Vikings are known for being scary invaders, they also lived in peace as farmers or sailed around Europe as traders.

Important Vikings had funeral ships that were sometimes set alight at sea.

Rich clothes, jewellery, weapons and even animals went in the ship with the dead person, and the ship was either buried or set alight at sea.

Some Viking ships had scary-looking dragons' heads carved on the front.

The first person to go up into space was Yuri Gagarin in 1961.

The cosmonaut (astronaut) from the Soviet Union (now Russia) travelled on the spacecraft Vostok 1 and spent 108 minutes orbiting Earth.

Valentina Tereshkova was the first woman in space, in 1963.

She had been a keen parachute jumper from an early age, which helped her qualify to become a cosmonaut. She flew in Vostok 6 and was in space for 2 days, 23 hours and 12 minutes.

**Today people visit space and
live there for months at a time, on the
International Space Station (ISS).**

**Astronauts on the ISS eat
Christmas dinner twice!**

Some have their festive feast on 25 December,
others on 7 January (Russian Christmas),
but some like to join in both.

The gaboon viper has a deadly disguise, blending in perfectly with dead leaves on the forest floor.

The snake, which has the longest fangs of any venomous snake, is completely hidden while it waits for prey to come along. Using colour to blend into surroundings is known as background camouflage.

Monarch butterflies, on the other hand, want to be seen.

Their bright orange-and-black markings are a danger signal that tells potential predators: "Don't eat me – I am poisonous."

Lots of other animals use bright colour in this way, too.

Red, orange, yellow and black are common warning colours.

Camels can go for months without drinking water.

They can cool their body down without sweating, so they don't lose water that way, and there is hardly any water in their breath. When they do find some water to drink, they drink a LOT.

There is a beauty pageant for camels in Dubai, United Arab Emirates.

Thousands of camels compete and millions of dollars are given out in prizes.

Australia is home to around a million camels.

They were introduced in the 19th century and thrive in Australia – but they cause problems, especially because they drink so much water.

Mobile phones are dirtier than toilets!

Several studies have found around 18 times more bacteria on a phone screen than on a toilet flush handle. Yuck!

Farts in jars were once used to try and cure plague victims.

In the 1600s, people thought that diseases were caused by something called miasma, meaning 'bad air'. Some doctors thought that diluting this air with another smell would help. It didn't work!

If your blood vessels were all stretched out in one very long line, they would wrap around the world more than three times.

The total length of blood vessels in the human body is between 96,000 and 161,000km.

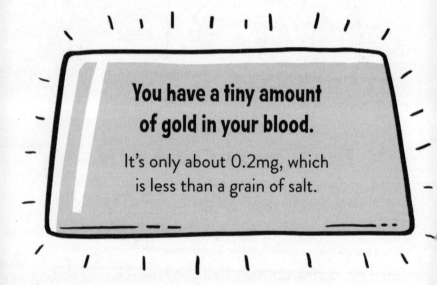

You have a tiny amount of gold in your blood.

It's only about 0.2mg, which is less than a grain of salt.

Not all blood is red.

Humans, other mammals, birds and most reptiles and fish have red blood. But beetles have yellow blood, earthworms have green blood, lobsters and squids have blue blood and some marine worms have purple blood!

Your heart will beat more than 3 billion times a lifetime.

That's 42,048,000 times a year for around 80 years.

At the North Pole, it is completely dark from the end of October until the end of January.

The sun disappears over the horizon in late September and there is a month of twilight before the sun sets for over 170 days.

**A man once swam for almost
19 minutes in the icy water surrounding
the North Pole – without a wetsuit!**

British swimmer Lewis Pugh completed this
swim in July 2007 to highlight the fact
that polar sea ice is melting.

The narwhal is called 'the unicorn of the sea'.

This whale, found in the cold Arctic Ocean, has a long, spiral 'horn' that can grow to over 3m long. It uses it to sense changes in temperature and chemicals in the seawater to help it find prey.

Hundreds of years ago, people thought a unicorn's horn could protect against poison.

In the 16th century, Queen Elizabeth I had one as an elaborate drinking cup. It was really a narwhal tusk.

The narwhal's 'horn' is a tusk, or tooth, that grows through its lip.

Narwhals cannot be kept in captivity.

Sadly, when they have been caught and kept in zoos they have quickly died. They need to be free!

Excited football fans caused an earthquake in Barcelona, Spain.

In 2017, a match between Barcelona and Paris Saint-Germain got really exciting. Barcelona was behind but scored several goals in the last minutes of the game.

With the final goal, the crowd went so wild jumping up and down that the ground shook, enough for earthquake scientists 500m away to record a mini-earthquake.

The manchineel tree is so poisonous that even sitting underneath it causes a painful rash.

The tree is found along the coasts of Florida, United States, and the Caribbean, and eating any part of it can kill you. Confusingly, it's also called the beach apple!

The world's most venomous animal is the Australian box jellyfish.

It has 15 tentacles that each contain about 5,000 stinging cells for zapping prey. It swims fast, unlike most jellyfish that just drift along.

Sliced bread was once banned in the USA.

The ban was during World War II and the aim was to save resources, including the thick waxed paper used to wrap the sliced bread. Sliced bread goes stale quickly, too. But so many people complained that the ban was lifted after two months.

Peanuts are not nuts.

True nuts, such as pecans and hazelnuts, grow above ground on trees. Peanuts grow in pods underground and are considered a legume – a group that includes peas, beans and chickpeas.

Fortune cookies do not come from China.

The famous cookies, baked with a paper strip inside, became popular in Japan in the 19th century. But they really took off after they were served in Chinese and Japanese restaurants in California, United States.

A young girl made some of the most important dinosaur discoveries ever.

Mary Anning grew up in Lyme Regis on the south coast of England in the 19th century. She made a living collecting and selling fossils and was the first to find skeletons of the prehistoric sea giants, ichthyosaurs and plesiosaurs.

In 2021, a toddler discovered one of the best-preserved dinosaur footprints ever.

Four-year-old Lily Wilder spotted the footprints on a beach in Wales. They turned out to be the footprints of an unknown dinosaur similar to *Coelophysis*, which was about as tall as an emu.

A dog's sense of smell is more than 10,000 times sharper than ours.

Noses contain pong-sensing cells called scent receptors. A dog has a lot more of these cells than a human does.

Some dogs can even sniff out when humans are ill.

They have the amazing ability to sense chemicals given off by people with several diseases including malaria, coronavirus and a few types of cancer.

A polar bear can smell its prey from 3km away.

Where the air is very cold, it's harder for smells to evaporate so they hang around. And polar bears have a very sharp sense of smell. They can even smell a seal through a metre of ice.

Some sand dunes sing or bark.

The mysterious sound happens when
wind blows over the dry sand of a desert.

A mountain in Africa is magnetic.

Kediet ej Jill mountain in Mauritania is made up almost entirely of magnetite, a magnetic rock. A compass won't be much help to anyone climbing the mountain, as the magnetite will stop it working.

Charles Lindbergh was the first person to fly SOLO non-stop across the Atlantic Ocean.

The American pilot set off from New York, United States, in May 1927 and landed near Paris, France, 33.5 hours later. He was in a plane called the *Spirit of St Louis*.

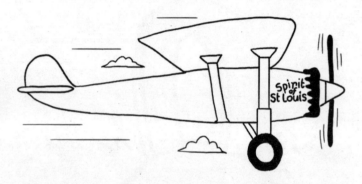

John Alcock and Arthur Brown had made the first non-stop flight eight years earlier.

The British airmen flew together from St John's, Canada, to Connemara, Ireland, in 16 hours 28 minutes in June 1919.

**A sheep, a duck and
a cockerel took a hot-air balloon
trip before any people did.**

The Montgolfier brothers from France
invented the hot-air balloon as a way
to travel. In 1783 they demonstrated
it with the animal passengers before
testing it with people a month later.

**Leonardo da Vinci designed
a helicopter way back in the
16th century, but it was never built.**

An oak tree does not produce acorns until it is at least 40 years old.

Oaks are mighty trees that take life slowly, often living for hundreds of years. Maybe it's not surprising that they don't produce their seeds for such a long time.

Bamboo on the other hand grows really fast – shooting up nearly 90cm a day.

It's the world's fastest-growing plant.

Coffee flowers give bees a memory buzz.

Coffee plants contain a substance called caffeine, which is what makes coffee perk people up. Bees feeding on coffee plant nectar get a quick boost to their memory and are more likely to remember to return to the same flower later.

Chocolate is a fruit.

Well, sort of. Cocoa pods are fruits that grow on the cacao tree. Inside the fruits are the seeds, or cocoa beans. These are dried, roasted and crushed to make yummy chocolate.

A woodpecker has an incredibly long tongue.

It uses it to slurp up insects from deep inside tree cracks. When it's not sticking its tongue out, it wraps it up in its head all the way behind its skull.

It drills into very hard wood without getting a headache.

The woodpecker has a thick spongy skull and strong neck muscles that together work like shock absorbers.

Crows are super-intelligent birds.

They have solved mazes and puzzles and passed memory tests with flying colours. They have even shown they can remember individual human faces.

You have more than five senses.

As well as sight, hearing, taste, smell and touch, you have a sense of balance, temperature, pain, hunger and thirst, and even the sense of knowing where all the parts of your body are without looking at them.

The human eye can see up to 10 million shades of colour.

We have colour-sensing cells called cones, which come in three types: red, green and blue. Amazingly, together these allow us to see all those different shades.

You can taste one teaspoon of sugar in almost 8l of water.

Sugary sweetness is one of five tastes along with salty, sour, bitter and umami (a savoury flavour).

The longest ever tennis match took 11 hours and 5 minutes.

The marathon match between John Isner of the United States and Nicolas Mahut of France was during the Wimbledon Championships in 2010. Isner won, and soon afterwards the rules were changed to prevent such a long, exhausting match happening again.

Light saber duelling is now an official sport in France.

The French Fencing Federation wanted to get more young people interested in the sport, so introduced a version using the famous *Star Wars* weapon.

Sometimes it rains frogs.

This happened in 2005 in Serbia, when thousands of frogs fell from the sky. They had probably been lifted out of ponds by a strong wind and then dropped far from home. They even survived the trip.

Freezing rain created an orchard of glass-like apples.

In Michigan, United States, in 2019, a farmer's apples were covered in ice after a storm. He shook the trees and some of the apples fell off, leaving perfect ice sculptures behind.